PLAY-POEMS OF
Robert Louis Stevenson

Where Go the Boats?

PICTURES BY
Max Grover

BROWNDEER PRESS   HARCOURT BRACE & COMPANY
San Diego / New York / London

Browndeer Press is a registered trademark of Harcourt Brace & Company.

Library of Congress Cataloging-in-Publication Data
Stevenson, Robert Louis, 1850–1894.
Where go the boats?: play-poems/by Robert Louis Stevenson;
illustrated by Max Grover.
p.   cm.
"Browndeer Press."
Contents: A good play—Block city—The land of
counterpane—Where go the boats?
ISBN 0-15-201711-9
1. Children's poetry, Scottish.   [1. Scottish poetry.]
I. Grover, Max, ill. II. Title.
PR5489.A3   1998
821'.8—dc21   97-9375

First edition   F E D C B A

Printed in Singapore

A
Good Play

We built a ship upon the stairs
All made of the back-bedroom chairs,
And filled it full of sofa pillows
To go a-sailing on the billows.

We took a saw and several nails,
And water in the nursery pails;
And Tom said, "Let us also take

An apple and a slice of cake"; —
Which was enough for Tom and me
To go a-sailing on, till tea.

We sailed along for days and days,
And had the very best of plays;
But Tom fell out and hurt his knee,
So there was no one left but me.

Block
City

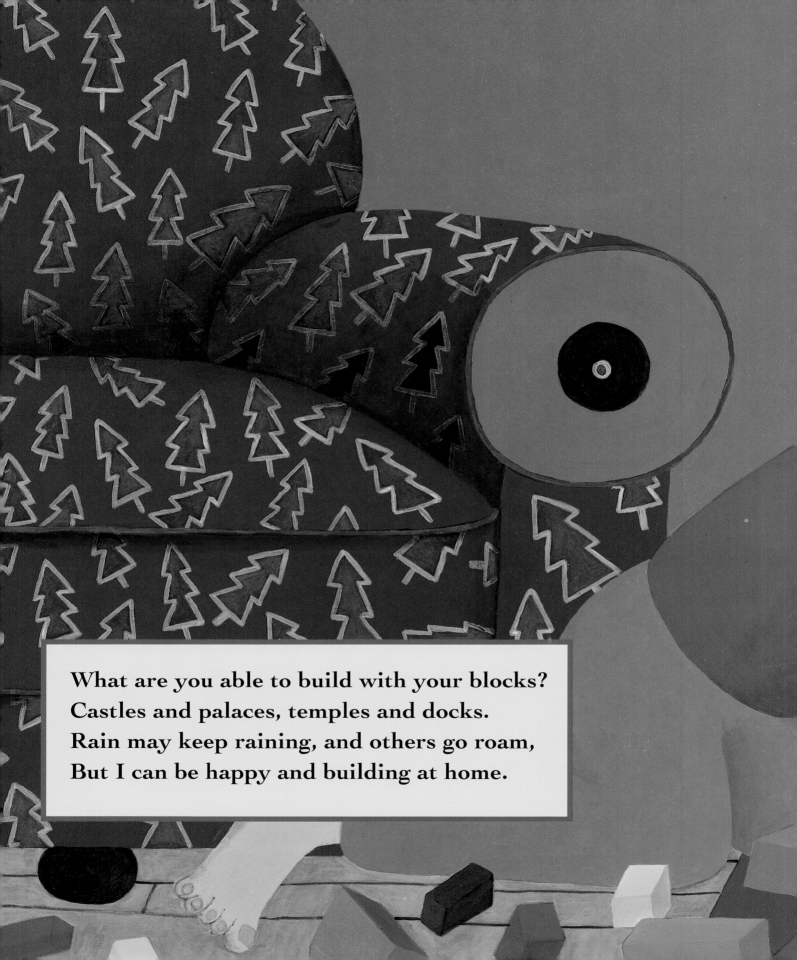

What are you able to build with your blocks?
Castles and palaces, temples and docks.
Rain may keep raining, and others go roam,
But I can be happy and building at home.

Let the sofa be mountains, the carpet be sea,
There I'll establish a city for me:
A kirk and a mill and a palace beside,
And a harbour as well where my vessels may ride.

Great is the palace with pillar and wall,
A sort of a tower on the top of it all,
And steps coming down in an orderly way
To where my toy vessels lie safe in the bay.

This one is sailing and that one is moored:
Hark to the song of the sailors on board!
And see on the steps of my palace, the kings
Coming and going with presents and things!

Now I have done with it, down let it go!
All in a moment the town is laid low.
Block upon block lying scattered and free,
What is there left of my town by the sea?

Yet as I saw it, I see it again,
The kirk and the palace, the ships and the men,
And as long as I live and where'er I may be,
I'll always remember my town by the sea.

The Land
of Counterpane

When I was sick and lay a-bed,
I had two pillows at my head,
And all my toys beside me lay
To keep me happy all the day.

And sometimes for an hour or so
I watched my leaden soldiers go,
With different uniforms and drills,
Among the bed-clothes, through the hills;

And sometimes sent my ships in fleets
All up and down among the sheets;
Or brought my trees and houses out,
And planted cities all about.

I was the giant great and still
That sits upon the pillow-hill,
And sees before him, dale and plain,
The pleasant land of counterpane.

Where Go
the Boats?

Dark brown is the river,
Golden is the sand.
It flows along for ever,
With trees on either hand.

Green leaves a-floating,
Castles of the foam,

Boats of mine a-boating—
Where will all come home?

On goes the river
And out past the mill,

Away down the valley,
Away down the hill.

Away down the river,
A hundred miles or more,

Other little children
Shall bring my boats ashore.

The illustrations in this book were done in acrylics
on D'Arches Lavis Fedilis drawing paper.
The display type was set in Cochin.
The text type was set in Cochin Bold.
Color separations by United Graphic Pte Ltd.,Singapore
Printed and bound by Tien Wah Press, Singapore
This book was printed on totally chlorine-free
Nymolla Matte Art paper.
Production supervision by Stanley Redfern
Designed by Camilla Filancia